NAVID'S STORY...

A **real-life** account of his journey from Iran

Created by
Andy Glynne
and Jonathan Topf

In memory of Katy Jones, without whom this project would have never been possible.

This paperback edition published in 2016
First published in hardback in 2015
Text and Illustrations © Mosaic Films 2015

Wayland, Carmelite House, 50 Victoria Embankment, London NW1 3BH

Mosaic Films, Shacklewell Lane, London E8 2EZ

Created by Andy Glynne
Illustrated and designed by Jonathan Topf

Editor: Debbie Foy
Layout design: Sophie Wilkins

Dewey ref: 362.7'7914'092-dc23

ISBN 978 0 7502 9286 3
eBook ISBN 978 0 7502 9373 0
Lib eBook ISBN 978 0 7502 7896 6

Printed in China

10 9 8 7 6 5 4 3 2 1

Wayland is a imprint of Hachette Children's Group,
An Hachette UK company.

www.hachette.co.uk
www.hachettechildrens.co.uk

NAVID'S STORY...

My name is Navid.

This is the story of my
journey from Iran.

WAYLAND
www.waylandbooks.co.uk

The reason that we left Iran was that my dad disagreed
with the Government and how things were going.

I remember a visit from some Government officials one day.
My dad's life was in danger and so he had to leave the country immediately

It was a similar story for many people
who were against the Iranian Government.

I suppose my
dad was lucky;
members of my
mum's family had
been executed
because they
were Kurdish.

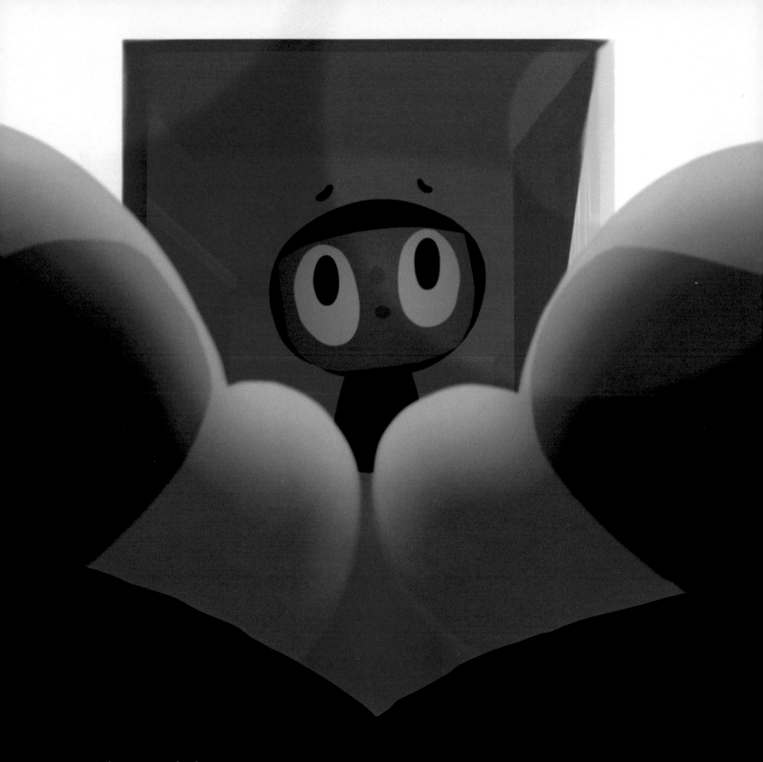

After he left,
the officials kept coming
back to our house to question my
mum about where my dad had gone.

We decided we
had to leave too.

I remember everyone was really
sad the night we left Iran.

At first I didn't understand
why they were sad, but when I
got to the airport I realised that I
was leaving my country for good. I
was upset for nearly the whole journey.

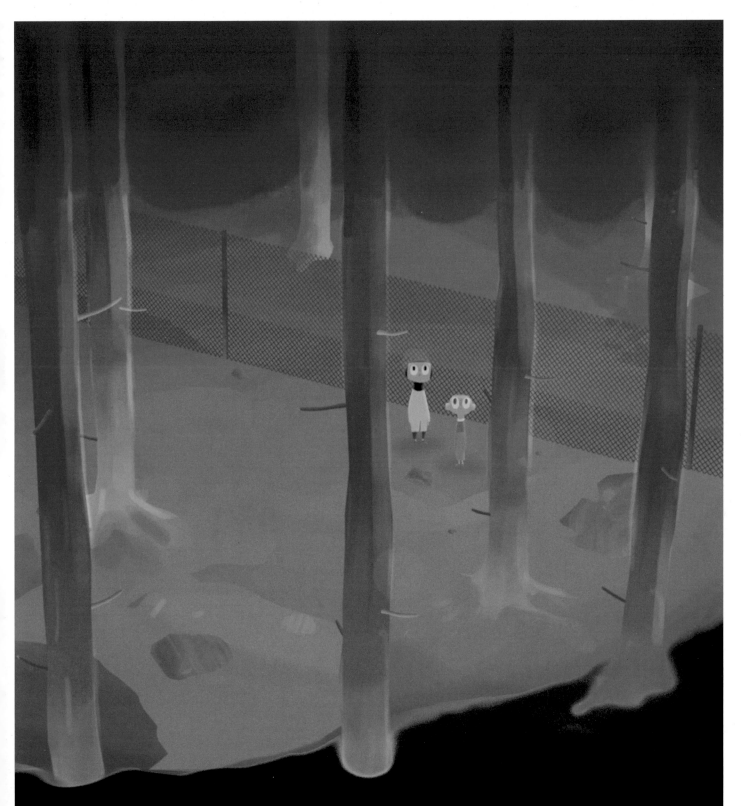

We flew to Italy and from there travelled mainly on foot.
We had to jump over a high wire fence, which was really scary.

We passed through a forest at night and got stopped by the local police. The sound of the police dog barking was terrifying.

I remember staying in a
      cottage one night.
            I think it was in Slovenia,
                  but I'm not sure.

The next night
when we had to
leave the cottage, I
was scared because
I could see the
concern on my
mum's face.

It was dark and uncomfortable.

I felt scared and really wanted to get out.

When we finally arrived in our new country, I remember someone cutting open the cover at the back of the lorry with a knife.

It was just like in the movies,
when the sunlight flooded in to show
my mum and I sitting there huddled
up at the back of the lorry.

When we got out of
the lorry the border
officials questioned
us, but they were
really friendly.

That was the day that I saw my dad for the first time in several years.

It was the weirdest thing because
it wasn't what I was expecting at all.

At first I didn't recognise him,
but then he explained that he was my
dad and how he'd missed me so much.

I remember sitting in the back of the car,
my mum and dad were in the front.

It was night time and I spent the whole
journey looking at him, trying to figure out
who he was and what was happening.

But gradually,

I became more and more comfortable around
him as I figured out that he was actually my dad!

I started school in my new country.
The first few days were really hard,
not because of the other students or teachers,
but just because I didn't know anything
– not even the language.

It was like being an outsider, and that was really scary for me.

One memory I have from school was when my mum would come to chat to me through the fence at break time.

When the bell rang to go back
to classes, my mum had to go home,
but I held on to the school fence as
though I was in some sort of prison.

I couldn't understand much of what was said to me at school. I just felt very lonely.

You could tell by their facial expressions that
people were being friendly, but not knowing what
they were saying was quite scary for me.

School was pretty difficult for me at first.

I had to learn to do everything.

At my school there was a wide variety of kids from different backgrounds.

There were other refugee kids at my school,
    and there was a centre you could go to after school
    to be with other kids in similar situations.

We could share our experiences and this was helpful for me.

So even though the first few months
were difficult, having that sense of
support was amazing for me.

And, of course, I had my mum and dad.